SERIES EDITOR Thomas S. C. Farrell

Social-Emotional Learning for English Language Educators

Luis Javier Pentón Herrera and
Grazzia María Mendoza Chirinos

bookstore.tesol.org

TESOL International Association
1925 Ballenger Avenue, Ste. 550
Alexandria, VA 22314 USA
www.tesol.org

Associate Director of Publications: Tomiko Breland
Copy Editor: Teddy Angert
Cover and Interior Design: Kathleen Dyson
Head of Education and Events: Sarah Sahr

Copyright © 2026 by TESOL International Association

All rights reserved. Copying or further publication of the contents of this work is not permitted without permission of TESOL International Association, except for limited "fair use" for educational, scholarly, and similar purposes as authorized by U.S. Copyright Law, in which case appropriate notice of the source of the work should be given. Permission to reproduce material from this book must be obtained from www.copyright.com, or contact Copyright Clearance Center, Inc., 222 Rosewood Drive, Danvers, MA 01923, 978-750-8400.

Every effort has been made to copyright holders for permission to reprint borrowed material. We regret any oversights that may have occurred and will rectify them in future printings of this work.

The publications of the TESOL Press present a variety of viewpoints. The views expressed or implied in this publication, unless otherwise noted, should not be interpreted as official positions of the organization.

Recommended citation:
Pentón Herrera, L. J., & Mendoza Chirinos, G. M. (2026). *Social-emotional learning for English language educators*. TESOL Press.

ISBN 978-1-953745-56-9
ISBN (ebook) 978-1-953745-57-6
Library of Congress Control Number 2025947835

Contents

Series Editor's Preface... v

Preface... vii

Chapter 1   What Is Social-Emotional Learning?................... 1

Chapter 2   Emotions and Identity in Language Learning.......... 9

Chapter 3   The Social Dimension of Social-Emotional
            Learning in Multilingual Classrooms................. 19

Chapter 4   Planning for Social-Emotional Learning
            With Multilingual Learners of English............... 29

Chapter 5   Embracing Social-Emotional Learning
            as a Pedagogy....................................... 37

References... 45

About the Authors.. 49

About the Series Editor.. 49

Series Editor's Preface

The English Language Teacher Development (ELTD) series consists of a set of short resource books for English language teachers that are written in a jargon-free and accessible manner for all types of teachers of English, including experienced and novice teachers. The ELTD series is designed to offer teachers a theory-to-practice approach to English language teaching, and each book offers a wide variety of practical teaching approaches and methods for the topic at hand. Each book also offers opportunities for teachers to interact with the materials presented. The books can be used in preservice settings or in-service courses and by individuals looking for ways to refresh their practice.

Pentón Herrera and Mendoza Chirinos's *Social-Emotional Learning for English Language Educators* explores different approaches to integrating social-emotional learning (SEL) into English language teaching practice that involves cultivating hearts, minds, and environments that nurture both intellectual and emotional intelligence. Luis and Grazzia provide a comprehensive overview of SEL as they explore practical strategies to embed SEL into curriculum planning and everyday classroom interactions to ensure the prioritizing of social-emotional growth and well-being as highly as academic achievement. As they note, SEL is not just an educational process but a crucial component of our pedagogical ethos. *Social-Emotional Learning for English Language Educators* is a valuable addition to the literature in our profession.

I am very grateful to the authors of the ELTD series for sharing their knowledge and expertise with other English language teaching professionals to make these short books affordable for all language teachers throughout the world. It is truly an honor for me to work again with each of these authors for the advancement of English language teaching.

Thomas S. C. Farrell

Preface

Dear readers: We are excited to welcome you to this journey of integrating social-emotional learning (SEL) into your teaching practice. As educators, our role extends beyond imparting academic knowledge; it involves cultivating hearts, minds, and environments that nurture both intellectual and emotional intelligence. This dual focus is essential in preparing students who are academically proficient, emotionally capable, and ready to meet the challenges of the world with resilience and empathy.

In this book, we delve into SEL as a tool for both teacher and student success. We explore practical strategies to embed SEL into curriculum planning and everyday classroom interactions, ensuring you prioritize social-emotional growth and well-being as highly as academic achievement. We encourage you to look at SEL as a cross-cutting pedagogy that becomes part of the education community. In our view, SEL can be an everyday exploration that follows varied pathways leading to fully shaping our learners.

As we dive into the complexities of SEL, we invite you to reflect on your own experiences and the pivotal role social-emotional dynamics play in your classroom. This is not just about enhancing educational outcomes but about enriching the lives of your students and your own professional fulfillment. We want you to be part of the journey that we, as educators, have started. We encourage you to engage in this learning and application, bringing adaptations to your contexts based on the local and global experiences we share. Most of the strategies, techniques, and suggestions you will find in this book are part of our journeys as practitioners, educators, and trainers. We hope they will help you as you connect to the needs and nuances of your context and consider which aspects fit your reality best.

CHAPTER 1

What Is Social-Emotional Learning?

> What good is increased access to education if it does not serve to make the world a more peaceful and connected community? (Morrell, 2018, p. ix)

Social-emotional learning (SEL) is at the heart of teaching and learning and provides the foundation for feelings of safety, confidence, and motivation. It involves teaching skills that are crucial for learner success both in the classroom and in life. In this first chapter, we aim to unpack the multifaceted nature of SEL and illustrate its critical role. Through this exploration, we will discover how SEL influences every interaction in the educational landscape and prepares students for both personal and academic challenges.

REFLECTIVE BREAK

Before we engage in defining and understanding what SEL is, we would like to begin this book and chapter with a few questions:

- Think back to a time when you felt particularly connected to your students—what emotions and/or social interactions shaped that moment?

- Take a moment to reflect on that memory. How did your actions or the dynamics in the classroom create an environment where trust and confidence could flourish?

- What can you learn from this memory, and how can you replicate those actions in your future teaching?

Your response to the first question is likely related to the relationships you built in the classroom space. Maybe you recalled a time when a student trusted you enough to share something personal, or perhaps you remembered a breakthrough moment when your encouragement helped a hesitant student engage more confidently.

These types of memories, where we felt particularly connected to our students, often stem from meaningful social and emotional exchanges, not just from academic achievements. For example, a simple moment of greeting a student warmly at the door or celebrating their small victories can create lasting bonds that reinforce trust and emotional safety. And if you ask your students, both present and past, about a time when they felt particularly connected to you or their classmates, they will probably share a story or anecdote where social and emotional exchanges were particularly important for them as well.

Rarely do teachers and students remember the exact content they learned unless it resonated emotionally, but the connections formed during meaningful interactions often stay with us forever, blending emotional connection with the learning experience. A famous quote (commonly misattributed to Maya Angelou) states that: "I've learned that people will forget what you said, people will forget what you did, but people will never forget how you made them feel" (Politico, n.d.). This wisdom applies directly to education, where meaningful social and emotional connections can shape memorable learning experiences and foster a deeper sense of belonging.

What Does SEL Look Like?

As teachers, we know that, at its core, teaching is relational. The way we make students feel heard, safe, and supported plays an essential role in their ability to learn. When students feel overwhelmed by stress, isolation, or fear of failure, a barrier called the affective filter can form. Language acquisition expert Krashen (1982) explained this filter as a mental block that hinders a learner's ability to process new information. Without lowering this affective filter, meaningful learning simply cannot take place. It's not just a *nice to do* strategy—it's essential for creating the conditions where language acquisition can occur. This is why creating an emotionally safe learning environment is crucial in the language classroom. When students feel calm, connected, and supported, their affective filter is lowered, allowing them to engage and take risks with language. *This is where SEL comes in.*

SEL is generally understood as the process by which individuals of any age develop and apply competencies to recognize and manage emotions, set and achieve beneficial goals, appreciate the perspectives of others, establish and maintain supportive relationships, make responsible decisions, and handle personal and interpersonal situations constructively. (Pentón Herrera, 2024b, p. 6)

In simple terms, SEL helps us build the skills needed to understand and manage our own emotions, develop empathy for others, strengthen our relationships, and make thoughtful, responsible decisions. It also reminds us that learning is inherently social; it happens in interaction with others and thrives in environments where social dynamics foster trust, respect, and collaboration.

For teachers, embracing SEL as part of our pedagogy means being aware of how our emotions and social interactions influence our teaching and being intentional about fostering helpful social dynamics in the classroom. For students, SEL creates a supportive space where they feel encouraged to take risks, express themselves, and learn collaboratively without the fear of failure holding them back. When students feel a sense of belonging and connection to their peers and teachers, they are more likely to engage actively in the learning process.

 REFLECTIVE BREAK

- Think about a time when a student shared feedback or a story that showed how much they valued the relational aspect of your teaching.
- How did this change the way you approach your interactions in the classroom?

In the language classroom, SEL can look like the following:

- Greeting students warmly and acknowledging their presence.

    Examples: *Hi, Maria, welcome to our class. Great to see you today!* Or: *Good morning, everyone! Before we start, I want to acknowledge that you're all showing up and doing your best, and I appreciate that very much.*

- Encouraging peer collaboration and promoting mutual respect during group activities.

    Examples: Before starting a pair activity, you might say: *Remember, the goal is to practice and support each other. If your partner makes a mistake, help them out and celebrate when you figure things out together.* Or: *During this activity, we are looking for constructive, not destructive, criticism and support. We are learning together and supporting one another.*

- Helping students reframe mistakes as opportunities for growth rather than reasons for embarrassment.

    Examples: After a student makes an error, respond with: *That was a tricky word, but I love that you tried! Let's break it down together.* Or: *Mistakes mean we're stretching our brains—this is exactly how language learning works!*

- Incorporating teacher stories to model SEL competencies.

    Examples: Share moments when you managed emotions, navigated challenges, or learned from social interactions: *One time, I felt really nervous presenting at a conference, but I reminded myself to take a deep breath and focus on connecting with my audience. That small action helped me stay calm and present.* Or: *When I was learning English, something that helped me during group discussions was reminding myself that making mistakes was part of the process. Instead of staying silent, I decided to ask questions, even if they weren't perfect. My teacher's encouragement and my classmates' support made me feel more confident—and I realized I learned more when I participated.*

- Addressing difficult situations.

    Examples: When encountering difficult situations like disrespect in the classroom, you can address it calmly but firmly by naming the behavior and explaining why it impacts the class: *I noticed there was some laughter while one of your classmates was reading. In this space, we support one another by showing respect and kindness. Let's take a moment to reset and show our classmates the same attention we'd want in return.* Alternatively, you can use reflective questions: *How do you think your words or actions affect others?* Or: *What can we do differently next time to make sure everyone feels respected and heard?*

When SEL practices are embedded into daily classroom routines, they don't just enhance classroom culture—they help lower the affective filter, making it easier for students to stay engaged and process new language. Pedagogically, SEL can be integrated at all levels, and the underlying premise backed by evidential research is that the sooner they are integrated into the classroom, the greater the influence on beneficial outcomes (Mendoza Chirinos, 2023). Ultimately, SEL supports the whole learner—and teachers!—reinforcing that language learning and teaching are not just academic processes but also part of a social and emotional journey.

 REFLECTIVE BREAK

- Think about your own classroom routines and interactions. What small but meaningful changes could you make to foster a more emotionally supportive environment?
- How might these changes affect your students' willingness to take risks with language learning?

SEL: Frameworks, Competencies, Activities

According to Pentón Herrera and Darragh (2024), when planning to include SEL, it is important to differentiate SEL frameworks, competencies, and activities. These terms are closely related but not interchangeable.

SEL frameworks are the overarching structures or foundations that guide the implementation of SEL within schools and classrooms. They provide comprehensive models and guidelines, defining the essential elements of SEL and suggesting how these can be embedded in teaching practices and school culture.

Some well-known examples of SEL frameworks are the CASEL framework (Collaborative for Academic, Social, and Emotional Learning [CASEL], n.d.) and the PATHS (Promoting Alternative THinking Strategies) framework (Education Endowment Foundation, 2015). CASEL outlines five core competencies—self-awareness, self-management, social awareness, relationship skills, and responsible decision-making—and PATHS focuses on emotional literacy, impulse control, and conflict resolution. To explore and learn more about various SEL frameworks, we recommend the Harvard EASEL Lab (exploresel.gse.harvard.edu).

SEL competencies refer to the specific social-emotional skills and abilities that SEL aims to develop in students. They are the targets or competencies teachers set to equip learners with the emotional intelligence and interpersonal skills necessary to navigate life both inside and outside the classroom.

Some examples of SEL competencies include *emotional regulation* (e.g., calming oneself during stressful situations), *empathy* (e.g., understanding a classmate's perspective), and *effective communicative skills* (e.g., expressing thoughts clearly while listening actively). Although some SEL competencies are universally important (e.g., empathy), teachers should consider which competencies are most relevant to their students' specific contexts. For example, in a conservative country, promoting self-regulation and respectful communication may be prioritized to align with cultural expectations around decorum and social interactions. On the other hand, in more open or progressive educational settings, there may be a stronger emphasis on fostering self-expression, emotional awareness, and advocacy to encourage students to voice their opinions and share their perspectives. For this reason, it's essential to prioritize competencies that will have the greatest impact on students' well-being and success.

Lastly, **SEL activities** are the concrete exercises and practices teachers use to help students develop SEL competencies. These are the day-to-day methods that make SEL real and actionable in the classroom. SEL activities are often hands-on, reflective, and student centered, encouraging students to apply their skills in authentic ways.

For example, to teach the SEL competency of self-awareness, students can write reflective poetry about an emotional experience. To do this, we can prompt students to think about a time when something happened that made them feel a particular emotion, then have them write a limerick, cinquain, haiku, free verse, couplet, or shape poem about it. To develop relationship skills and foster collaboration, they can participate in cooperative games where teamwork is essential, such as collaborative storytelling or two truths and a lie. To practice conflict resolution and build responsible decision-making skills, students can engage in role-playing exercises where they navigate real-life social scenarios, such as resolving disagreements during group projects or responding empathetically to peer criticism. For more examples of SEL activities in English language teaching, we recommend *Activities for Social-Emotional Learning* by Hasper and Pentón Herrera (2024).

We want to highlight that SEL is not a one-size-fits-all approach—it should be adapted to fit the unique needs of teachers, students, and their learning environments. In some classrooms SEL is integrated directly into lessons, with competencies taught alongside academic skills. For example, Pentón Herrera and Martínez-Alba (2021) offer a template for lesson plans that blend SEL and academic objectives seamlessly. In other settings, SEL may take the form of add-on activities, such as after-school programs or special initiatives. There are also contexts where SEL is taught as a standalone subject with its own lessons and assessments, similar to other academic subjects.

We also recognize that in some places the term "SEL" itself is not used because of political or religious sensitivities, as articulated by Pentón Herrera (2024b). In these contexts, teachers often reframe their work as promoting "21st-century skills" or "teaching the whole child." No matter how SEL is approached in your specific context, our hope is that you and your students engage with it in ways that are proactive, supportive, and safe for everyone.

 REFLECTIVE BREAK

- Is SEL present in your teaching environment? If yes, please outline it.
- In what ways could you begin—or expand—SEL practices to better support yourself and your students?

Conclusion

Now that we've established what SEL is and why it matters, the next step is to explore how emotions and identity shape the language-learning experience. In Chapter 2, we will look closely at the emotional dimensions of language learning, discuss strategies for fostering self-awareness and emotional regulation, and reflect on language learning as a deeply personal and identity-shaping process. As you engage with this book's content, we invite you to think about ways in which SEL will support you in establishing helpful interactions in the classroom. Also, consider the ways in which SEL is integrated through a cross-cutting approach to support your teaching, especially as you dive into Chapter 2 and consider the emotions within SEL.

CHAPTER 2

Emotions and Identity in Language Learning

> Emotions can facilitate or impede children's academic engagement, commitment, and ultimate school success since relationships and emotional processes affect how and what we learn. (Cristóvão et al., 2017, p. 2)

Picture this: You are teaching English to a group of adult learners, and Sabrina—a former nurse in her home country—sits quietly, her hands fidgeting as she searches for the courage to speak. In her native language she could comfort patients, explain complex procedures, and navigate life with confidence. In English, however, the words come slowly, wrapped in hesitation and delivered in a timid tone. Each attempt feels like a vulnerable step toward reclaiming her voice—a reminder of how different she sounds compared to her true self. For Sabrina, language is not just about grammar and vocabulary; it is her bridge to connect with others and an expression of her identity. You can see the conflict in her eyes: the pride of her past expertise and the frustration of not yet being able to express it fully in this new language.

 REFLECTIVE BREAK
- How can we help students like Sabrina feel empowered rather than alienated in the classroom?
- What would it look like to build a classroom community where language learning fosters pride in personal narratives?

Two well-known proverbs that reflect the deep connection among language, emotions, and identity are, "To have another language is to possess a second soul," (a proverb often attributed to Charlemagne) and, "The limits of my language mean the limits of my world," by philosopher Ludwig Wittgenstein (1922, p. 74). These sayings highlight that language is more than just a means of communication—it shapes how we understand ourselves and interact with the world around us. For multilingual learners of English (MLEs), language learning is not just an academic journey but an emotional and personal one (e.g., as seen through Sabrina's eyes in the preceding vignette). It involves navigating new cultural landscapes, expressing one's identity in different ways, and experiencing both the excitement and the vulnerability that come with speaking in another language. In this chapter, we will explore how the emotional dimensions of social-emotional learning (SEL; i.e., emotions and identity) intersect in the language-learning process and how teachers can foster a supportive classroom environment where MLEs feel safe, valued, and empowered.

First, let's begin with an invitation to reflect on your own language learning experiences. If you have not had experience learning a new language, you can reflect on your own learning trajectory more generally. By reflecting on your own experiences, you may uncover insights that can inform your teaching practices and help you create a classroom where your MLEs feel understood and supported.

 REFLECTIVE BREAK

- Can you recall a time when you were learning a language other than your first language, or a specific content/topic that was of great interest to you?
- What motivated you to learn that language or content/topic?
- What emotions did you experience while learning that language or content/topic, and what factors contributed to those feelings?
- Would you describe your learning experience as meaningful and successful? What factors made the journey rewarding or challenging?

SEL in Second Language Learning

In formal education and language teacher preparation programs, we are often taught to approach language education in methodical and pragmatic ways, focusing on lesson plans, grammar structures, and measurable outcomes (Richards, 2013). However, the reality is that language learning—and teaching—extends far beyond the pages of textbooks. As language teachers, language learners, and language users, we know languages live and breathe in our everyday experiences: in quiet moments of self-reflection and inner dialogue, as well as in dynamic interactions with the world around us.

Acknowledging this reality opens the door to understanding the deeply personal nature of language learning and teaching. When we recognize that language learning is embedded in both social and emotional exchanges, we create space to view language not just as an academic subject but as a core part of one's identity and lived experience. This shift in perspective invites us to consider how our teaching practices can support MLEs in expressing their authentic selves and navigating their learning journeys with the resilience and confidence essential for two key language-learning elements, persistence and engagement. This broader understanding of language learning also leads us to reimagine our classrooms as spaces where academic growth, emotional development, and social identity formation coexist and support one another. When viewed through an SEL lens, language education has the potential to become more than the transmission of linguistic knowledge—it becomes a process of nurturing the whole learner and contributing to a better world.

In practice, the focus of language education often tilts heavily toward academic growth with the assumption that success in this area will naturally foster emotional well-being and identity development. However, this is not always the case. Students may excel academically or have unimaginable academic potential while still feeling disconnected or anxious in the classroom. To cultivate a truly supportive learning environment, we must intentionally address all three dimensions (academic, emotional, and social) in balance. Here's why each element is essential.

- **Academic growth:** This involves the development of linguistic skills such as reading, writing, speaking, and listening. While academic growth is measurable through assessments, it thrives in environments where students feel empowered to take risks and make mistakes (Honigsfeld, 2024). Without emotional support, academic progress can feel overwhelming and unattainable for students.

- **Emotional development:** Learning a language can evoke a range of emotions including excitement, fear, pride, and frustration (see Pentón Herrera & Trinh, 2021, for examples). Supporting students' emotional development means helping them build resilience, manage anxiety, and celebrate their progress. We know undesired or adverse emotions can act as barriers to language acquisition, potentially leading to demotivation and even language learning attrition if left unaddressed (Horwitz, 2001).

- **Social identity formation:** Language learning is deeply tied to identity. It shapes how students see themselves and how they express their unique perspectives (Norton, 2013). In the process of acquiring a new language, students may feel a sense of in-betweenness, feeling caught between cultural expectations as they navigate cultural differences and negotiate their identities. A classroom that values self-expression and cultural diversity creates a space where students feel seen, respected, and included.

When academic growth, emotional development, and social identity formation are prioritized in harmony, students are more likely to succeed academically while also developing confidence, self-awareness, and a sense of belonging (Pentón Herrera & Darragh, 2024). Balancing these three core elements of teaching is at the heart of SEL practices. As teachers, we have the opportunity to intentionally design lessons and interactions that nurture the whole learner, fostering a classroom culture where academic achievement becomes a natural outcome of holistic growth. In Figure 1, we show a visual representation of how these three elements work in unison, illustrating the core of SEL practices.

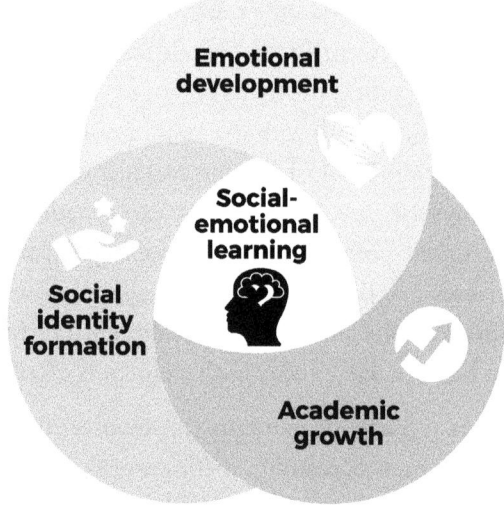

Figure 1. The three core elements of social-emotional learning in language learning.

REFLECTIVE BREAK

How can you balance these three elements in your teaching practice?

- **Academic growth:** How do you create opportunities for your students to mobilize their linguistic repertoires in ways that feel achievable and meaningful? Are there moments when the pressure to meet academic goals may unintentionally overshadow emotional or social needs?

- **Emotional development:** In what ways do you support your students' emotional well-being during the learning process? How do you help them build resilience and confidence, especially when they encounter challenges or setbacks?

- **Social identity formation:** How do you create a classroom environment where students feel seen, heard, and valued for their unique identities and perspectives? Are there ways you could further foster a sense of belonging and inclusivity?

Emotional Intelligence: A Key Outcome of SEL

One of the many benefits of SEL is that it supports the development of teachers' and students' emotional intelligence (EI). Mayer and Salovey (1997) define EI as the ability to "perceive accurately, appraise, and express emotion; the ability to access and/or generate feelings when they facilitate thought; the ability to understand emotion and emotional knowledge; and the ability to regulate emotions to promote emotional and intellectual growth" (p. 10). To be emotionally intelligent means to recognize your own emotions and the emotions of others and to use this understanding to guide your actions, reactions, and interactions. It involves knowing when emotions may be affecting your performance, using emotions as valuable information, and practicing self-regulation to stay calm and focused during challenging situations.

In the classroom, EI is critical for language teachers—especially novice language teachers—as our emotions are intrinsically connected to our teacher performance and our physical and emotional well-being (Pentón Herrera & Martínez-Alba, 2022). Emotionally intelligent teachers can recognize their own emotional triggers and employ strategies such as deep breathing, reframing unhelpful thoughts, or pausing before reacting to maintain composure during challenging moments. This self-awareness allows them to stay calm and respond thoughtfully rather than reactively. Teachers with high levels of EI are also better equipped to recognize and respond to the emotional needs of their students. For example, an emotionally intelligent teacher may notice when a student appears anxious about speaking in front of their peers and adjusts their approach by offering encouragement or reducing performance pressure. Teachers with strong EI foster student-centered, empathetic learning environments where students feel supported and valued rather than controlled. This creates a classroom culture that promotes self-discipline, cooperation, and a sense of belonging (Tok et al., 2013).

For students, developing EI involves building self-awareness, understanding their emotions, and recognizing how these feelings affect their learning process. Emotionally intelligent students can identify when emotions such as frustration, embarrassment, or anxiety are affecting their ability to speak, listen, read, or write in English. They can then use strategies such as deep breathing, visualization, or positive self-talk to manage these emotions and stay engaged (Reyes et al., 2012). This emotional awareness empowers them to persevere through challenges and take academic risks, even when they feel vulnerable. For example, a student who feels nervous before a presentation may acknowledge their anxiety and use calming techniques to participate actively rather than shutting down or avoiding the task altogether. When students develop EI, they are better equipped to navigate the ups and downs of language learning with resilience and confidence, fostering both academic growth and a stronger sense of agency (Pentón Herrera, 2024c).

In language learning, EI plays a crucial role in fostering resilience and self-efficacy by helping students recognize and manage the emotions associated with the language acquisition process. Students who feel comfortable acknowledging their frustration after making a mistake are more likely to persevere; such a growth mindset allows them to view setbacks as opportunities for growth rather than signs of failure. Think of a time when you struggled to communicate in a different language: How did you feel, and what helped you push through? Moments like these remind us that when we embrace our emotions and learn from them, progress becomes possible.

By contrast, those who suppress or ignore their emotions may experience heightened anxiety, reduced confidence, and eventual disengagement—a reality we all face at times. Can you recall a moment when fear or frustration held you back from participating, even though you had something valuable to say? In our classrooms, we might observe this when students hesitate to participate because of feelings of anxiety or uncertainty, or when they become overly self-critical or frustrated with their mistakes and impatient with the gradual pace of language learning. This illustrates how emotional barriers can prevent learners from sharing their thoughts and reaching their potential, both in the classroom and beyond.

For this reason, it is essential for language teachers to create an EI-rich environment for themselves and their students. EI is not only vital for language teaching and learning but also for navigating our daily interactions, whether at home, at work, or in our communities. After all, communication nearly always happens through language. By fostering EI, we empower students to express themselves with confidence, embrace mistakes as valuable learning opportunities, and build meaningful connections with the world around them.

As a final point, EI is closely tied to how students form and express their social identities. Language learning can evoke complex feelings related to self-worth, belonging, and cultural pride. MLEs, especially those migrating to a new country, may feel torn between multiple cultural identities, navigating the expectations of their heritage culture and the culture of the language they are learning. By placing EI at the center of their practice through SEL, teachers can create a safe classroom environment where students feel validated and understood (Pentón Herrera, 2024a). For instance, incorporating culturally responsive materials and activities affirms students' backgrounds and invites them to share personal stories that foster connections with peers.

Strategies to Support Emotionally Intelligent Multilingual Learners of English

A growing number of studies of SEL in English language teaching are finding that academic success and emotional well-being are interconnected, signaling future best practices in the field (McGovern & Yeganeh, 2024; Rutledge & Manegre, 2024).

The following activities will help support emotionally intelligent MLEs while creating an inclusive and emotionally supportive classroom environment. More specifically, we share examples of activities and strategies to support MLEs' emotions, identity development, and academic growth.

Emotions

A strategy that is key for setting the stage for learning as the day begins is check-ins (Mendoza Chirinos, 2023). Check-ins can influence the mood of the day by creating a safe learning space and an optimistic outlook on what the rest of the time at school will look like. For younger learners, special greetings such as high fives or happy dances can make entering the classroom a joyous moment. For adolescent and adult learners, displaying a thought-provoking question on the board to spark discussion or playing an uplifting song as they enter are effective ways to engage them right from the start.

Although check-ins are vital, the importance of SEL extends beyond initial classroom interactions and is especially crucial during times of global stress, such as the COVID-19 pandemic or conflicts between or within countries. In Honduras, for example, video comics incorporating local cultural elements and SEL themes such as empathy and resilience were developed (Development Alternatives Incorporated [DAI], 2021a). These educational comics also served as emotional support, reaching more than 2.1 million learners across various media platforms nationwide. This innovative approach underscores the essential role of EI in assisting students as they navigate complex and challenging circumstances effectively.

Identity Development

An essential element of SEL is identity exploration and building, which plays a crucial role in helping MLEs develop the social-emotional competencies of inclusion, tolerance, empathy, and critical thinking. To promote identity exploration and building, educators can create interactive scenarios that encourage MLEs to share their personal perspectives, drawing from their backgrounds, life experiences, and cultural contexts. Teachers can facilitate this by creating stories or using traditional and well-known stories where learners collaborate to propose alternative endings that are constructive, inclusive, or ethically nuanced.

Another effective activity for exploring identity involves using role-play to simulate real-life situations. This technique allows students to adopt various social roles and perspectives, helping them understand diverse viewpoints and navigate social interactions. Through role-playing, learners can critically examine their own beliefs and biases, fostering a more profound sense of empathy and enhancing their interpersonal skills. Such activities not only strengthen self-awareness and value understanding but also contribute significantly to building self-worth among students.

Academic Growth

Academic growth can be reached through varied pathways. One way to do this could be through the integration of peacebuilding into English language instruction, which enhances academic achievement by creating an engaging and collaborative classroom environment. Educators can integrate the concepts of peacebuilding into lessons by encouraging students to apply new language skills in discussions about conflict resolution, empathy, and cooperation (DAI, 2021b). To do this, students might need sentence starters, a list of phrases that are conducive to conflict resolution and/or peacebuilding, or other scaffolds. For example:

- How can we find a solution to this problem?
- Please, help me understand _____.
- It's important that we both feel respected. What steps can we take?
- How can we address this conflict so everyone benefits?

Another pathway to follow in order to deepen linguistic capabilities and cultivate essential social skills consists of building a community of practice as described in Principle 6 of TESOL's *The 6 Principles for Exemplary Teaching of English Learners: Grades K–12* (TESOL International Association, 2024), where educators engage in application and collaborative efforts among educators, students, and educational stakeholders, ensuring that learning environments are both supportive and conducive to academic growth. These two pathways can build strong foundations for learner academic growth and success.

Conclusion

In this chapter, we explored the emotional dimension of SEL, focusing on the concepts of emotions, identity, and academic growth. In Chapter 3, we will delve deeper into the social aspect of SEL, highlighting how it enriches interactions and learning in multilingual classrooms.

CHAPTER 3

The Social Dimension of Social-Emotional Learning in Multilingual Classrooms

> I came to the realization that nearly all the social and emotional behaviors students need to learn are best developed through effective classroom management, group and partner work, and questioning. (Ribas et al., 2018, p. 2)

Picture this: Ms. Kowalska, the teacher, has prepared a class that focuses on vocabulary about textures and clothing. She has provided textured materials to help bring the story to life for all her students, including those who are visually impaired. As the class reads through the description, Layla, who is visually impaired, sits beside her buddy Marco. He gently guides her hands over different fabrics that represent the textures described in the book: the rough burlap of sacks, the smoothness of fresh tomatoes, and the sticky sweetness of spilled honey. Marco also attempts to convey the colors of the textures using temperatures and sensations; he describes the red of tomatoes as being warm as the sun and yellow as light and airy as a breeze. This sensory-based approach helps Layla visualize the scene but also deepens the learning experience for Marco, teaching him to appreciate and describe nuances he had never considered before.

REFLECTIVE BREAK

- How do you ensure that all students, especially those with disabilities, are actively involved in the learning process?

- In what ways do you prioritize socialization in your learning context? What does it look like?

Prosocial Skills: A Key Outcome of SEL

Scholars and educators alike agree that all learning is a social—and emotional!—activity (Frey et al., 2019). Vygotsky (1986) explained this in his sociocultural theory, stating that the sociocultural experience of individuals, or the "outside factors" (p. 94), including socialization, affects our development, thought, and language. For many multilingual learners of English (MLEs), particularly in cultures that highly value community and social interaction, learning and using a language is inherently a social process. For these learners, isolated study sessions may not be as effective for language acquisition. In this chapter, we explore how teachers can create a classroom environment that supports students' prosocial skills, such as empathy, cooperation, cultural competence, and effective communication, which have been identified by the World Economic Forum (2025) as essential competencies for the 21st-century workforce. These skills are behaviors that promote helpful social interactions and relationships and are essential for building a supportive and inclusive classroom environment. We will delve into strategies that enhance these areas and discuss how they contribute to building a cohesive and supportive learning community.

 REFLECTIVE BREAK

- Reflect on a recent teaching moment where empathy played a key role. How did understanding your students' perspectives change the outcome of that lesson?

- How do you facilitate and encourage cooperation among your students?

- What strategies have you found most effective for improving communication skills within your classroom?

- In what ways do you provide spaces for the multicultural backgrounds of your students to be highlighted?

As language teachers, we are keenly aware that the essence of language is inherently social; it is crafted, evolved, and learned within the context of human interactions. Languages exist because of and for human interaction. Recognizing the social nature of language can transform our pedagogy and classroom dynamics. For MLEs, social-emotional learning (SEL) is particularly crucial as it supports them in navigating their emotional worlds while becoming part of the diverse social environments around them. To enhance interpersonal skills, encourage collaboration, and foster a sense of belonging, language teachers need to craft activities that move away from engaging in learning in isolation, such as learning grammar rules or vocabulary separately, focusing only on worksheets or language drills. Becoming aware of integrating SEL into education requires the understanding that it encompasses several processes. It is necessary to engage in:

- managing emotions;
- goal setting;
- showing empathy;
- addressing conflict resolution in positive ways;
- engaging in positive behaviors; and
- making responsible decisions.

Social Considerations Within SEL

Within the social dimension of SEL, we find several aspects we should consider in our classrooms. Among these are interpersonal skills as the foundation for establishing successful communication and relationships (California Department of Education, 2024). MLEs come from diverse cultural backgrounds with diverse linguistic repertoires and bring their own set of challenges in expressing themselves and understanding their peers. Supporting MLEs in interpreting social cues, such as body language, tone, and facial expressions, is key to enhancing interpersonal interactions. Moreover, group dynamics can become a barrier for MLEs due to their lack of understanding of unfamiliar group norms or expectations (Mendoza Chirinos, 2023). Fostering inclusion and providing support to help them collaborate, acknowledge differences, and recognize the value of diverse perspectives helps learners navigate these dynamics (Jagers, 2018). Finally, social inclusion is a vital part of allowing learners to feel valued and supported in a learning space where all cultural contributions are valued, equitable participation is enabled, and MLEs are actively involved in all discussions and activities.

As English language teachers, we need to consider that there are many nuances that influence language use and communication in social interactions, and it's crucial for our students to understand these to become effective communicators. For instance, body language, which varies significantly depending on the social and cultural context, is as integral to communication as spoken language itself. Similarly, concepts such as silence—which may be viewed as awkward in some cultures and valuable in others—or the tone, volume, and emphasis of our voices also play critical roles in how our messages are perceived by listeners.

The significance of societal norms and cultural contexts in communication is profound. These deeply ingrained elements shape not only how messages are conveyed but also how they are interpreted across different social landscapes. Recognizing and adeptly navigating these nuances is crucial for developing affective communicative competence, which enhances effective cross-cultural interactions. As detailed by Pentón Herrera and Darragh (2024), affective communicative competence goes beyond simply understanding and managing one's own emotions in communication; it also encompasses the ability to perceive and react appropriately to the emotions of others within diverse cultural settings. This skill is vital for educators and students alike as it facilitates deeper, more empathetic connections and fosters a more inclusive learning environment.

Ten Social Dimension Considerations

Following, we share 10 nonexhaustive considerations within the social dimension of SEL that we, as language teachers, should take into account. Each consideration is accompanied by sample exercises that can be used to address each consideration.

1. **Body language:** Includes gestures, facial expressions, and posture, which can convey various meanings, such as agreement, confusion, or discomfort. A suggested activity is to have students in small groups research body language in their culture and then present their findings, reflecting on the use of the gestures and the varied interpretations.

2. **Tone of voice:** Influences how messages are perceived, whether as aggressive, caring, or indifferent. A suggested exercise is preparing

a script of one or two short phrases and having students practice reading the sentence in varied tones, such as caring, aggressive, interested, or indifferent. Students can reflect on the tone and message conveyed.

3. **Volume:** Can imply confidence, anger, or excitement, varying in appropriateness depending on the cultural context. A suggested task could entail speaking in different volumes, such as low, normal, or loud, and having peers take notes of how each volume makes them feel. This can be followed by a discussion on cultural perceptions and appropriateness.

4. **Silence:** May represent respect, contemplation, or disapproval, with interpretations differing widely across cultures. Introducing scenarios of silence or role-playing could be relevant strategies for demonstrating when silence is used and what messages each situation provides regarding context and cultural interpretations.

5. **Eye contact:** Signals attention and respect in some cultures, while it can be considered disrespectful in others. In pairs, learners take turns speaking and listening while deliberately maintaining eye contact. Afterward they can discuss how eye contact influenced their connection.

6. **Personal space:** Varies culturally; proximity can signal familiarity and comfort or be seen as intrusive. Using measuring tape or string and markers, measure and mark personal space. Learners discuss how the boundaries are different depending on their culture and how the proximity affects comfort and interaction.

7. **Touch:** Can communicate support or comfort, but may be considered inappropriate in many educational and cultural settings. Practice high fives, handshakes, and pats on the back and discuss what they each mean. Learners discuss their levels of comfort with each and the cultural perceptions influencing their backgrounds.

8. **Emphasis (either with words or body language):** Highlights certain words, which can change the message's intent and urgency. Similar to tone or volume, practice emphasizing different words in a sentence, and have learners discuss how meaning shifts or is altered in each instance.

9. **Gestural communication:** Can have different meanings in different cultures (e.g., nodding or shaking the head). Learners draw varied gestures they are familiar with and their meanings. Through a walking gallery, they visit each other and reflect on their own meanings and insights for each gesture based on their cultural backgrounds.

10. **Facial expressions:** Are often universal, but the contexts in which they are appropriate can vary. In pairs, learners take turns expressing varied emotions through different facial expressions. Later, they reflect on each expression, discussing the meaning and making cultural references if applicable.

REFLECTIVE BREAK

After reading the preceding 10 nonexhaustive considerations within the social dimension of SEL, reflect on the following questions:

- What activities could you introduce to your class to help students explore and understand the role of body language and tone in different cultural contexts?

- Can you think of a recent lesson where incorporating discussions about cultural variations in communication (such as the use of silence or personal space) might enhance student understanding and empathy? How would you structure this lesson?

Three Key Prosocial Skills

In addition to the various social elements and aspects connected to communication, another important focus of SEL when it comes to the social dimension is the development of prosocial skills. Prosocial skills are not just desirable traits but essential competencies that support individuals throughout their lives, including during developmental years in school and during adulthood in today's labor force (World Economic Forum, 2025). These skills enable MLEs to engage meaningfully with their peers, understand diverse perspectives, and contribute to their community. Within multilingual classrooms prosocial skills become even more critical as they bridge cultural and linguistic divides and foster a sense of belonging and mutual respect among students from various backgrounds. In the subsections below, we focus on three prosocial skills that we believe are essential in language teaching and learning: empathy, cooperation, and effective communication.

Empathy

Empathy, one of the most critical social-emotional competencies, is the cornerstone of prosocial behavior, as it allows MLEs to perceive and react to the emotional states of others. In language learning, empathy enhances the ability to understand and use language in a way that is sensitive to the cultural and emotional contexts of communication partners. It also allows MLEs to be sensitive to their environment, reacting both verbally and nonverbally in ways that respect and acknowledge the feelings and cultural nuances of those around them—a hallmark of effective communicators. When teaching empathy in the English language classroom, it is crucial for educators to consider how they can foster an environment where students feel safe to express their emotions and explore the perspectives of others. This involves creating a classroom culture that values diversity and encourages open dialogue about the cultural and emotional dimensions of language use, enabling students to better understand and empathize with the experiences and feelings of their classmates.

Cooperation

Cooperation, an essential facet of prosocial skills, extends beyond simple group tasks to encompass the ability to navigate and respect diverse social norms and communication styles. In multilingual classrooms, cooperation is critical as it enables MLEs to work effectively with peers from varied backgrounds and fosters a classroom environment that values collective effort and mutual respect. Being able to collaborate with others gives MLEs the ability to engage constructively in tasks that require them to integrate multiple viewpoints and cultural insights, thereby enriching their learning experience. When fostering cooperation in the English language classroom, educators should consider how to cultivate a classroom climate that emphasizes the importance of shared goals and mutual support among students. This involves promoting an understanding that effective collaboration goes together with respecting individual differences and leveraging these to enhance group dynamics. Such an environment supports language development while also preparing MLEs to operate successfully in diverse teams, reflecting the interconnected nature and demands of today's global and multicultural society.

Effective Communication

Effective communication is crucial in multilingual classrooms, encompassing more than the simple exchange of information. It involves the ability to articulate ideas and emotions clearly and to listen actively, which is foundational for successful interactions in any language. This skill is particularly important in diverse settings both inside and outside educational spaces, as it includes sensitivity to nonverbal cues and the capacity to adjust communication styles to meet the varied linguistic and cultural backgrounds of individuals.

When promoting effective communication in the English language classroom, educators need to consider the comprehensive nature of communication skills. This encompasses not only the words used but also how they are spoken, as well as accompanying nonverbal cues that can vary significantly across different cultures. Teachers should focus on creating a supportive environment where students feel valued and listened to and where they can practice these skills in real-time interactions. Furthermore, it is essential for educators to model effective communication practices themselves, demonstrating how to interpret and convey subtle nuances in language that respect and reflect diverse cultural norms. This modeling helps students understand and apply similar patterns in their own interactions, enhancing their overall communicative competence.

Figure 2 presents a summary of the nonexhaustive considerations within the social dimension of SEL in this chapter.

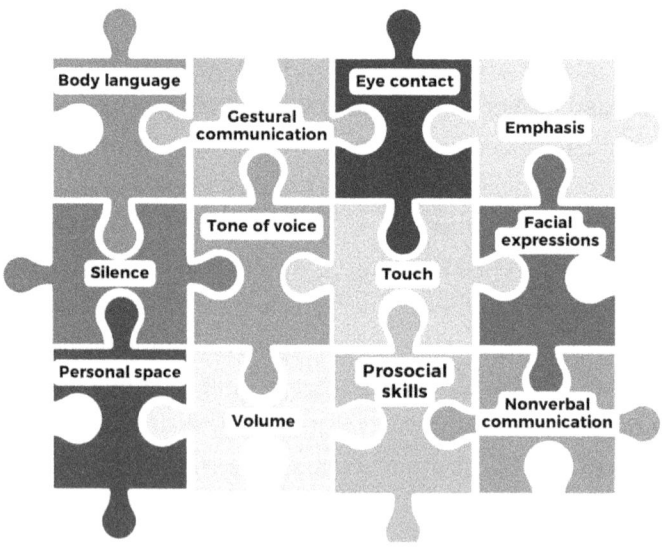

Figure 2. Some considerations within the social dimension of social-emotional learning.

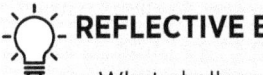 **REFLECTIVE BREAK**

- What challenges have you encountered in fostering an environment that promotes open and effective communication among students with different linguistic and cultural backgrounds?
- How have you addressed these challenges?

Strategies to Support the Prosocial Skills of Multilingual Learners of English

In this section, we share practical strategies that can help MLEs develop empathy, cooperation, and effective communication skills, as these are touchstones of social-emotional competencies in the social dimension of SEL.

Empathy

There are many ways in which we can foster empathy, ranging from perspective-taking activities, storytelling, emotion journals, and mapping. These activities involve role-playing to share opinions, building characters with different motivations and feelings, keeping a daily note of emotions, and outlining emotions linked to varied scenarios, respectively.

An example of an activity could be where learners in groups are assigned a specific scenario, such as welcoming a new student, disagreeing about a specific class activity, or giving their opinion on a class situation. Students organize themselves and act out the scenario, focusing on expressing empathy through gestures, facial expressions, volume, body language, tone, and specific actions. When the skit is completed, the group can discuss how empathy was shown.

Cooperation

To promote cooperation, activities could include collaborative projects focusing on specific goals or community service projects that involve students volunteering in their communities. Also, engaging in mindfulness practices, including meditation, deep breathing, and yoga allows students to self-regulate and be self-aware while respecting others' space. Additionally, engaging in open discussion or conversation/compassion circles, taking turns speaking and listening about challenges and issues, and coming up with solutions together can help build a supportive classroom environment.

A sample activity is a collaborative circle project where students engage in active listening, offering perspectives and effective communication. Learners sit in circles and use challenging situation scenarios to express their feelings about the situation, their opinion, their experience (if any) with a similar situation, and potential solutions to the challenge. Then, learners can role-play the solutions and emotions involved. A creative exercise within the activity would be drawing the scenarios and solutions and organizing a gallery walk. The circle is closed through a reflection process emphasizing the relevance of supporting others, active listening, and valuing others' perspectives.

Effective Communication

Workshops are great tools to support SEL integration as they provide learning by doing: hands-on experiences to engage in developing SEL core competencies. There should be a focus on each communicative activity to enhance effective communication.

An example could be listening and providing feedback. For this, set the stage at the beginning of the workshop by using videos and demonstrations related to effective communication, active listening, and positive feedback that help build supportive environments. Through discussion cards in small groups, learners take turns discussing each prompt on the cards. Afterward, they take on the roles of listener, speaker, and those who provide feedback. The emphasis will be on the beneficial aspects of communication and providing helpful ways to improve areas that need improvement. To close the workshop as a whole group, the learners can come up with their own communication guidelines and post them in an area of the classroom to keep in mind.

Conclusion

In this chapter, we have delved into the social dimension of SEL, examining how prosocial skills such as empathy, cooperation, and effective communication are integral to fostering a supportive and inclusive learning environment in multilingual classrooms. We also explored practical strategies and activities that can help educators cultivate these skills among students, enhancing their ability to interact effectively across diverse cultural and linguistic backgrounds. In the next chapter, we will discuss how to integrate SEL into your teaching practice, discuss considerations when integrating SEL, and share some ideas and templates for lesson plans that can be adapted to your context.

CHAPTER 4

Planning for Social-Emotional Learning With Multilingual Learners of English

> At the heart of culturally responsive teaching is instruction that supports students in becoming critical, self-directed learners who can bring all of themselves to learning. (Snyder & Staehr Fenner, 2021, p. 107)

By now, we hope you have a greater understanding of social-emotional learning (SEL), including the connections among education, language learning, and emotional aspects. It's time to plan for its integration! In this chapter, we will explore approaches to planning, provide sample lessons, and guide you into thinking about integrating SEL into your practice, school, and community.

We ask you to consider integrating SEL into your teaching practice and embedding it in everything you do within your classroom and school, with the understanding that your practices trickle into the community sustainably and progressively. As you engage in the proposed guideline, keep in mind your context and the needs, interests, families, and community of your multilingual learners of English (MLEs). We have mentioned that integrating SEL is dependent on the nuances of where the teaching and learning process takes place and is not a one-size-fits-all approach. We invite you to think of SEL as a systematic approach that fosters the necessary "conditions for everyone to build trusting and collaborative relationships, rigorous and meaningful curriculum and instruction, and ongoing evaluation" (CASEL, 2021. p. 1).

REFLECTIVE BREAK

- What would a holistic approach to academic growth and SEL look like in your specific context?
- What specific SEL competencies (e.g., empathy, growth mindset) would benefit your learners the most and why?
- How can you become an advocate for SEL and build agency among your MLEs so they become advocates within their communities as well?

Integrating SEL Into Your Practice

Let's consider several aspects to embed SEL into your teaching practice. We need to go step by step, considering: the curriculum, unit planning, lesson planning, and extracurricular activities.

For the curriculum, consider what content would allow SEL to integrate more naturally in your context and think strategically about the content that will require more work and buy-in. For your unit planning, think about those topics and themes that can be specific to developing SEL core competencies and which are the ones that will allow ongoing practice by the learners, as well as space for reflection and analysis. For your lesson, consider in which of the steps you can make links to self and where the connections to others can be made. Think about the activities that are closely related to important issues or topics for you, your students, and your context, such as conflict resolution, decision-making, or awareness of the behaviors of self and others, and how this can lead to reflective extension activities. Finally, for your out-of-classroom activities, think about which SEL core competencies or behaviors you would like to see implemented beyond your classroom, such as specific greeting habits within the school with peers and school staff. Similarly, consider which are those you wish to promote among families and the community, such as caring for the environment or supporting those in need.

REFLECTIVE BREAK
- What are some of the most immediate needs and behaviors that need to be addressed in your classroom?
- What is the level of awareness of SEL within your school and within your community?
- What are the bridges that connect your SEL work in your classroom and school with the community?

Integrating SEL into education requires clarity, as there is no specific recipe nor are there unique guidelines or steps for all contexts. It has to be viewed with the understanding that each context will require its specific adaptations and unique processes. Considering this and based on culturally responsive pedagogy, we need to view SEL as a transformative approach "whereby students and teachers build strong, respectful relationships founded in the appreciation of similarities and differences, learn to critically examine root causes of inequity, and develop collaborative solutions to community and societal problems" (Jagers et al., 2018, p. 3).

Planning an SEL Lesson

With this in mind, let us consider what an SEL lesson could look like and follow a simple lesson format: warm-up, introduction, activity or activities, reflection, and closure. During the introduction, you set the stage and catch the learners' attention. Identify which social-emotional competencies you want to focus on; in this example, let's say you want to help students develop conflict resolution skills. Your introduction could start with "I can" statements: Begin the lesson by letting each of your learners provide short statements of things they can do. This sets a proactive environment focused on the awareness of your and your learners' capabilities. Take note of what each can do and then link these together into "We can" statements connecting what they all can do as a community. This leads learners to think beyond the individual and consider the strengths of a group.

Now, we can move to the activity or activities. It could be reading a short narrative or a more extended literary passage on conflicts where the characters can't seem to find an answer, and they find themselves at a crossroads. The learners can act as advisors, proposing through drawings different ways to solve the conflict. They do this in pairs, which are organized based on their "I can" statements. They set up a walking gallery to display their work and explain their drawings. Next, reflect on all the proposed solutions and students' thought processes. At this stage, you can also ask if the dilemma resonates with them or someone they know. Finally, for closure, engage the learners in a process where they list what they are capable of achieving individually and as a team, offer potential solutions to solve the conflict, and think about how empathy plays a role in supporting others to solve conflicts.

 REFLECTIVE BREAK

- What are the approaches, techniques, or strategies you find most helpful when integrating SEL?
- Which SEL competencies do you plan to focus on and why?
- How do you plan to set up the activities: individually, in groups, or a combination of the two? Why?

Sometimes, following an SEL template helps us set up and adapt our own lessons. Following, we share a template that addresses a lesson related to culturally responsive pedagogies, collaborations, and connecting SEL to language learning. This is an example of a lesson that could take a week or more, depending on the frequency and length of your classes, but that can be divided into short excerpts to do each day. It can help you craft your own lessons by adapting as you move into the journey of a cross-cutting approach to integrating SEL into your practice.

A Sample SEL Lesson

Lesson Title: Who Has the Right of Way?
Grade Level: 5–8 and High School

Learning Objectives	Materials and Resources (Printed or Digital)
- To analyze a situation by reviewing a scenario - To reflect on how cultural background can influence decision-making - To collaborate through brainstorming to provide a solution to the scenario - To integrate the vocabulary learned the previous week related to giving directions **SEL Competency:** Conflict Resolution	- Scenario - Infographic templates - Case study templates - Cardboard boxes and cardboard for street signs - Colored flashcards (different unique designs based on the number of students in your classroom) - Masking tape
Preparation for Warm-up Activity (Preclass Preparation) 1. With small cardboard boxes and tape, create avenues and streets. (The boxes are buildings along the avenues and streets.) 2. Create pertinent street signs by searching the internet for street sign images you can print. **Warm-up Activity** 1. Prepare students to understand the meaning of right of way by presenting either visuals or a video. 2. Learners situate themselves along the city you have created in the classroom. 3. Each learner represents a driver in a vehicle; give each of them a card with a different color on it. 4. Make up a story that allows the learners to follow paths along the streets following the street signs, considering the cultural aspects of driving and recognizing the rights of others aligned with their own obligations as drivers. The intent of the warm-up is to distinguish traffic rules and signs, reflect on what is culturally relevant in a specific context or contexts, and consider the respect needed when driving in a community. This will set the stage for decision-making during the main activity. Be creative in naming the streets, connecting them to SEL. For example: Decision-Making Avenue, Empathy Street.	

Planning for Social-Emotional Learning With Multilingual Learners of English

Main Activity

Provide students with the following conflict scenario and have them collaborate to resolve the conflict. You can include visuals, provide note-taking templates, and assign roles within the groups of students you organize.

Scenario

There are four cars that have arrived at an intersection at almost the same time, with only seconds of difference among them. This is a four-way stop intersection, meaning all cars must stop before moving forward, and they cross the street based on the order in which they arrive at the intersection. Due to the almost simultaneous arrival, the drivers decide that each of them has the right of way first. This reasoning makes them all move along at the same time, causing an accident between two of the vehicles.

You are a mediator, and your task is to collaborate with your group to support the drivers involved in the accident to find a healthy solution and prevent the other drivers from adversely influencing the situation. Note that drivers come from different parts of the world.

Closing and Assessment

As a whole group, respond:

- What did you learn today?
- How did you integrate the vocabulary into the lesson?
- How is this vocabulary relevant to real life?
- Why was it helpful to be working as a group of mediators rather than working individually?
- What should the city do to prevent this type of situation from happening in the future?

Reflection – Gallery Walk

- Through infographics, learners share:
- How did they feel when deciding who had the right of way?
- What is the role of the mediator in a conflict?
- What would they advise someone in a mediating role?
- How can language become an important tool for mediation?

Extension Activity

- Learners create their own scenarios.
- Create a scenario booklet you can use for future activities.

Take Home Action

Have learners journal about conflicts they see in their community. Ask them to observe only; they don't intervene. Have them take notes on:

- Type of conflict
- Who is involved (adults, children, relatives, friends)
- Is the conflict resolved? Why or why not?
- During the week, they can choose to share with you (their teacher) or peers

 **REFLECTIVE BREAK**
- What do you think of this lesson plan?
- Could this be something you could integrate into your context as is?
- Could this be a lesson you can adapt, completely or in part?
- Think about the ways a similar lesson could be crafted for your context and which areas you would keep or tweak.

Conclusion

In this chapter, we explored the components of a lesson and different activities or techniques we could use to set the stage for ongoing practice and learner reflection. Techniques are varied and include storytelling as an SEL tool to bring relevant reflection to the learning space, as well as changing endings to promote critical thinking influencing decision-making, awareness of self, and awareness of others. Role-playing, skits, and readers' theatre to support empathy can also lead learners to understand equitable and inclusive practice when learning, collaborating, interacting, and being part of their school and their community.

Integrating SEL holistically into your teaching practice can lead to empowering learners. For example, Rogers (2024) exemplifies how, in an Asian context, culture plays a determining role in all aspects of life. In this case, focusing on learners as a whole can empower them to build agency and promote active learning, allowing them to find their voices. However, no matter the lesson or approach you choose based on your context, integrating SEL will make a difference in how your learners will begin to view the world around them and how they influence it.

We invite you to reflect on the information you have learned here as you read Chapter 5 and begin embracing SEL as a pedagogy.

CHAPTER 5

Embracing Social-Emotional Learning as a Pedagogy

Education is a process of living and not a preparation for future living. (Dewey, 1897, p. 78)

If you are reading this book and have reached this chapter, it means you are either an English language teacher or someone who is interested in improving the lives of multilingual learners of English (MLEs). As an advocate for MLEs, at some point in your professional life you probably wondered about (or found) your *why*. That is, *Why am I a teacher or someone who advocates for MLEs?* In this final chapter we will delve deeper into that question, reflecting on the criticality of moving beyond seeing social-emotional learning (SEL) as a practice and embracing it as a pedagogy—as part of who we are and what we do in our teaching and in our lives.

REFLECTIVE BREAK
- What is the purpose of learning an additional language?
- How can SEL improve language teaching and learning?

Education and SEL

For many of us, being a teacher is both a calling and a manifestation of our deepest convictions about what it means to contribute to society. By now, we are aware that what we do in the classroom extends beyond mere content delivery; it shapes the lives of our learners and has a direct impact on their academic learning and personal growth. This means we are teaching to nurture and interact with the whole person. When students come to us, they come as individuals who are experiencing hardships, successes, challenges, and victories in their personal and academic lives. As their teachers, our role begins as we get to know our learners and understand their backgrounds, context, and what they bring to the classroom. It entails getting to know our students as more than learners; we see them as the whole and complex human beings we know they are (TESOL Writing Team, 2024).

This is why, in our view, SEL is not just an educational process but a crucial component of our pedagogical ethos. SEL allows us to reach into the human aspect of education, thereby informing and transforming the learners we encounter and, in the process, ourselves. Embracing SEL as a pedagogy means weaving it into the very fabric of your educational philosophy. And if you are doing it well, it may naturally percolate into your own personal life, as often our personal and professional teacher lives are closely intertwined.

If we agree that SEL is about "understanding and information around feelings and sensibilities derived by pleasant companionship with others" (Turner, 2024, p. 15), then we can agree that a core element of SEL is well-being. Well-being is a prerequisite to healthy relationships with ourselves and others, and one of the most critical factors contributing to our quality of life and success. As such, embracing SEL as our pedagogy means establishing practices that protect and prioritize well-being in our teaching and in our lives. We propose that SEL pedagogy for well-being must, then, be proactive, responsive, reflective, and protective. In Figure 3, we share a visual representation of these four practices.

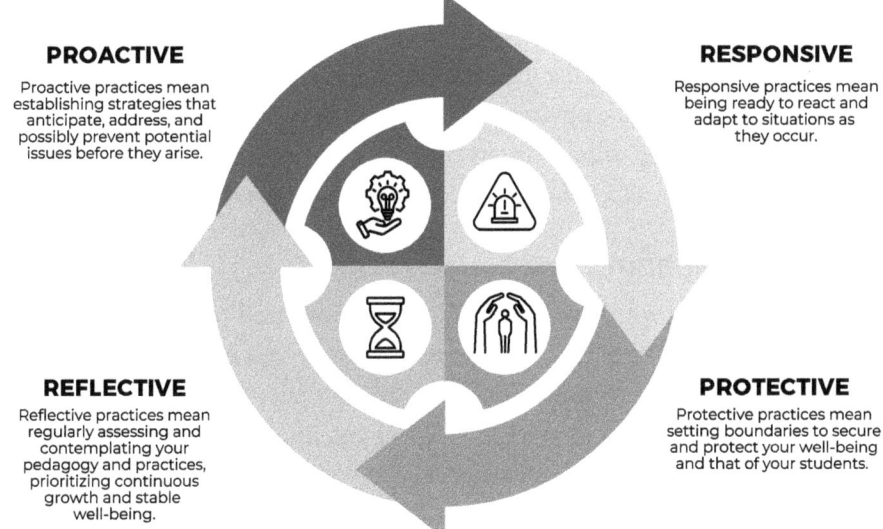

Figure 3. Four practices of SEL pedagogy.

 REFLECTIVE BREAK

As you consider the integration of SEL into your educational philosophy, take a moment to reflect on your current teaching practices:

- **Proactivity:** In what ways do you proactively create a classroom environment that anticipates and supports the social-emotional needs of your students? How do you positively influence your context beyond the classroom to promote prosocial change and healthy connections?

- **Responsivity:** How do you respond to unexpected challenges or emotional crises in the classroom? Are your responses helping foster resilience and understanding?

- **Reflection:** How often do you reflect on your teaching practices and their impact on your and your students' well-being? What have you learned from these reflections? How do you model reflection for your MLEs?

- **Protection:** What boundaries and protective measures have you established to safeguard the emotional health of both yourself and your students? What actions have you and your peers taken to make your school a safe space for learning?

SEL Pedagogy for Well-Being

In this section, we explain the practices shown in Figure 3 in more detail, proposing that SEL pedagogy for well-being demands practical application and commitment. We believe that as educators, we must embed these four principles into every facet of our professional practice and personal growth.

Proactive Planning

Proactive planning within SEL pedagogy transcends traditional lesson preparation, embedding itself into the very ethos of how educators perceive their role and interact with their students. This broader understanding involves anticipating and strategically addressing the social-emotional needs that influence student learning and development across all school interactions, not just in specific lessons. By viewing every interaction as an opportunity to support our and our students' development, educators can create a nurturing environment that shapes students' attitudes toward learning and their interpersonal interactions.

To put this into practice, consider the school environment as a whole: from the physical space, which should feel welcoming and safe, to the informal interactions that occur outside structured class time. Proactive planning might involve creating quiet corners for reflection or collaboration zones that encourage cooperative learning. It extends to teacher training sessions that focus on recognizing signs of emotional distress or social withdrawal and offering strategies for supportive intervention. Moreover, proactive planning means viewing each day as an opportunity to model and reinforce the values and behaviors we hope to instill in our students. This could include deliberate strategies such as integrating themes of empathy, respect, and community into every school event, from assemblies to sports days, ensuring that SEL is continuously reinforced in both word and action.

Responsive Action

Responsive practices in SEL pedagogy emphasize the importance of educators' ability to adapt and respond effectively to their and their students' social-emotional needs as they arise. This dynamic component of SEL pedagogy is about more than merely reacting to challenges; it involves a thoughtful adjustment of teaching methods, communication styles, and behavioral strategies in real-time, ensuring that responses are attuned to the diverse and fluctuating needs of the classroom. By being responsive, educators can manage classroom dynamics more effectively, providing immediate support or intervention that helps maintain a stable, balanced, and supportive learning environment.

Implementing responsive practices means being observant and sensitive to cues our bodies or our students provide, whether they are verbal or nonverbal. For example, a sudden change in a student's behavior might require a quick but careful approach to ascertain the cause and provide the necessary support. This could range from a private conversation to adjustments in classroom activities that acknowledge and address the student's emotional state. Additionally, responsive practices include fostering an environment where everyone, including you, the teacher, feels safe expressing their feelings and knows that their voices will be heard and respected. This might involve spontaneously adapting lesson plans to tackle emergent social issues that affect your or students' well-being or modifying classroom discussions to allow more time for students to process and speak on emotionally charged topics.

Reflective Practice

Reflective practices in SEL pedagogy involve a continuous cycle of self-assessment and contemplation of one's teaching strategies, interactions, and overall well-being. This introspective approach enables educators to consider the effectiveness and sustainability of their teaching methods. By regularly reflecting on their practices, educators can ensure they are consistently aligning with SEL principles and making necessary adjustments to enhance educational outcomes, personal development, and balanced practices that equally prioritize professional engagement and personal well-being.

In practical terms, reflective practices include routine check-ins with ourselves and, when possible, with our colleagues or students. Reflective practices could involve journaling about daily teaching experiences, discussing challenges and successes in peer groups, or even formal sessions with a coach or supervisor. These reflective sessions should focus on questions such as: *How did my teaching today align with SEL principles? What impact did my interactions have on my and my students' well-being? How did today's experiences affect my own emotional state?* Engaging in continuous reflective practices allows us to become more emotionally intelligent educators who view continuous growth and lifelong learning as a way to prioritize our well-being (Farrell, 2018, 2020).

Protective Measures

Protective practices in SEL pedagogy are about establishing clear boundaries that safeguard both the educator's and the students' well-being. These measures ensure the educational environment remains a place of safety and respect, where social-emotional needs are met without compromising personal integrity or comfort. By setting and maintaining these boundaries, educators help foster a culture of mutual respect and understanding that is essential for effective SEL implementation. Protective measures also serve as models for students, teaching them how to set their own boundaries and respect those of others, a critical component of social-emotional competence, emotional intelligence, and success.

Implementing protective measures can involve creating explicit practices that address respect for personal space, managing appropriate levels of emotional sharing, and defining clear lines of communication among students and between students and teachers. For educators, it might mean establishing professional limits, such as appropriate times for student contact and preventing burnout by ensuring there is a balance between availability and personal time. Protective practices should also include strategies for dealing with emotional overload, such as having a support system in place or knowing when to seek help from mental health professionals. This could be facilitated through regular training on mental health awareness as well as having access to available resources that empower educators to take action when they or their students need additional support. Although we understand these practices might be easier said than done, we want to emphasize their value in protecting and enriching the learning environment, making it a supportive and sustainable space for everyone involved.

 REFLECTIVE BREAK

- How could embracing an SEL pedagogy influence your own well-being and that of your students?

- Can you identify a moment this week where you practiced proactive, responsive, reflective, or protective SEL strategies? What was the outcome?

Conclusion

We would like to end this final chapter and this book by recognizing that embracing SEL as a pedagogy is not merely about adopting a set of practices; it's about cultivating a mindset that values and actively promotes the holistic and sustainable development of all individuals within the educational sphere. And yes, this means teachers, students, and the community alike. This journey requires commitment, reflection, and a willingness to continually evolve. It requires a mindset shift and allowing this shift to spread beyond our classrooms. It comes with an important responsibility to build safe spaces for learning where everyone is recognized and heard, and where they belong.

Our pathways into SEL begin within ourselves and our pedagogy, influencing our classrooms, schools, and, eventually, our communities. SEL is a way of being, living, and perceiving life and what surrounds us. If we allow it, SEL can also be a set of guiding principles, a way of learning and living for us and for our learners' academic and personal growth and success.

References

California Department of Education. (2024). *Transformative SEL conditions for thriving*. https://www.cde.ca.gov/ci/se/tselconditions.asp

Collaborative for Academic, Social, and Emotional Learning. (CASEL). (2021). *The CASEL guide to schoolwide SEL essentials*. (3rd Edition). https://schoolguide.casel.org/content/uploads/sites/2/2019/09/2021.6.15_School-Guide-Essentials.pdf

Collaborative for Academic, Social, and Emotional Learning. (CASEL). (n.d.). *What is the CASEL framework?* https://casel.org/fundamentals-of-sel/what-is-the-casel-framework/

Cristóvão, A. M., Candeias, A. A., & Verdasca, J. (2017). Social and emotional learning and academic achievement in Portuguese schools: A bibliometric study. *Frontiers in Psychology*, *8*, 1913. https://doi.org/10.3389/fpsyg.2017.01913

Development Alternatives Incorporated. (2021a) *School based violence activity quarterly report 2*. USAID, Honduras

Development Alternatives Incorporated. (2021b) *School based violence activity quarterly report 3*. USAID, Honduras.

Dewey, J. (1897). My pedagogic creed. *School Journal*, *54*, 77-80. http://dewey.pragmatism.org/creed.htm

Education Endowment Foundation. (2015). Promoting alternative thinking strategies (PATHS). https://files.eric.ed.gov/fulltext/ED581278.pdf

Farrell, T. S. C. (2018). *Reflection-as-action in ELT*. TESOL Press.

Farrell, T. S. C. (2020). *Reflective teaching* (Rev. ed). TESOL Press.

Frey, N., Fisher, D., & Smith, D. (2019). *All learning is social and emotional: Helping students develop essential skills for the classroom and beyond*. ASCD.

Hasper, A., & Pentón Herrera, L. J. (2024). *Activities for social-emotional learning: Developing social-emotional competences in the ELT classroom*. Delta.

Honigsfeld, A. (2024). *Growing language and literacy: Strategies for secondary multilingual learners*. Heinemann.

Horwitz, E. (2001). Language anxiety and achievement. *Annual Review of Applied Linguistics, 21*, 112–126. https://doi.org/10.1017/S0267190501000071

Jagers, R. (2018). *Why we can't have social and emotional learning without equity.* Learning Is Social and Emotional. https://schoolguide.casel.org/uploads/sites/2/2019/05/Jagers-Equity-Blog-.pdf

Jagers, R., Rivas-Drake, D., & Borowski, T. (2018, November). *Equity social and emotional learning: A cultural analysis* [Frameworks brief]. WestEd. https://drc.casel.org/uploads/sites/3/2019/02/Equity-Social-and-Emotional-Learning-A-Cultural-Analysis.pdf

Krashen, S. D. (1982). *Principles and practice in second language acquisition.* Pergamon Press.

Mayer, J. D., & Salovey, P. (1997). What is emotional intelligence? In P. Salovey, & D. J. Sluyter (Eds.), *Emotional development and emotional intelligence: Educational implications* (pp. 3–34). Basic Books.

McGovern, K., & Yeganeh, V. (2024). Devised drama as social-emotional learning. *Anglica. An International Journal of English Studies, 33*(1), 19–41. https://doi.org/10.7311/0860-5734.33.1.02

Mendoza Chirinos, G. (2023). Supporting learners' social emotional learning. In V. Canese & S. Spezzini (Eds.), *Teaching English in global contexts: Language, learners and learning* (pp. 88–97). Editorial Facultad de Filosofía, UNA. https://doi.org/10.47133/tegc_ch06

Morrell, E. (2018). Foreword. In N. Mirra, *Educating for empathy: Literacy learning and civic engagement* (pp. ix–x). Teachers College Press.

Norton, B. (2013). *Identity and language learning: Extending the conversation.* Multilingual Matters. https://doi.org/10.21832/9781783090563

Pentón Herrera, L. J. (2024a). An agenda for emotional intelligence in language teacher education. *Language Teacher Education Research, 1*, 48–63. https://eurokd.com/doi/10.32038/lter.2024.01.03

Pentón Herrera, L. J. (2024b). Introduction to social-emotional learning in English language education: Mapping the landscape and reflecting on the way forward. *Anglica. An International Journal of English Studies, 33*(1), 5–18. https://doi.org/10.7311/0860-5734.33.1.01

Pentón Herrera, L. J. (2024c). Social-emotional learning in ESOL with ninth-grade newcomers. *ELT Journal, 78*(2), 127–136. https://doi.org/10.1093/elt/ccad051

Pentón Herrera, L. J., & Darragh, J. J. (2024). *Social-emotional learning in English language teaching.* University of Michigan Press.

Pentón Herrera, L. J., & Martínez-Alba, G. (2021). *Social-emotional learning in the English language classroom: Fostering growth, self-care, and independence.* TESOL Press.

Pentón Herrera, L. J., & Martínez-Alba, G. (2022). Emotions, well-being, and language teacher identity development in an EFL teacher preparation program. *Korea TESOL Journal, 18*(1), 3–25. https://koreatesol.org/sites/default/files/pdf_publications/KTJ18-1web.pdf

Pentón Herrera, L. J., & Trinh, E. T. (Eds.). (2021). *Critical storytelling: Multilingual immigrants in the United States*. Brill /Sense. https://doi.org/10.1163/9789004446182

Politico. (n.d.). *Getting there: Maya Angelou*. https://www.politico.com/story/2014/05/getting-there-maya-angelou-107195

Reyes, M. R., Brackett, M. A., Rivers, S. E., White, M., & Salovey, P. (2012). Classroom emotional climate, student engagement, and academic achievement. *Journal of Educational Psychology*, *104*(3), 700–712. https://doi.org/10.1037/a0027268

Ribas, W. B., Brady, D., & Hardin, J. M. (2018). *Social-emotional learning in the classroom: Practical guide for integrating all SEL skills into instruction and classroom management*. Ribas.

Richards, J. C. (2013). Curriculum approaches in language teaching: Forward, central, and backward design. *RELC Journal*, *44*(1), 5–33. https://doi.org/10.1177/0033688212473293

Rogers, B. (2024). Using English language teaching as a platform for developing self-advocacy: English is our future. In K. Mastruserio Reynolds, G. M. Mendoza-Chirinos, D. Suarez, O. Effiong, & G. Kormpas (Eds.), *Decentering advocacy in English language teaching: Global perspectives and local practices* (pp. 116–133). University of Michigan Press.

Rutledge, E., & Manegre, M. (2024). An emotionally intelligent, ecolinguistic approach to content and language integrated learning. *Anglica. An International Journal of English Studies*, *33*(1), 109–124. https://doi.org/10.7311/0860-5734.33.1.06

Snyder, S., & Staehr Fenner, D. (2021). *Culturally responsive teaching for multilingual learners: Tools for equity*. Corwin.

TESOL International Association. (2024). *The 6 principles for exemplary teaching of English learners: Grades K–12* (2nd ed.). TESOL Press.

Tok, T. N., Tok, S., & Dolapçioğlu, S. D. (2013). The relationship between emotional intelligence and classroom management approaches of primary school teachers. *Educational Research*, *4*(2), 134–142. https://www.interesjournals.org/articles/the-relationship-between-emotional-intelligence-and-classroom-management-approaches-of-primary-school-teachers.pdf

Turner, W. (2024). *Embracing adult SEL: An educator's guide to personal social emotional learning success*. Routledge.

Vygotsky, L. (1986). *Thought and language* (Rev. ed.). The MIT Press.

Wittgenstein, L. (1922). *Tractatus logico-philosophicus*. Kegan Paul, Trench, Trubner & Co.

World Economic Forum. (2025). *The future of jobs report 2025*. https://www.weforum.org/publications/the-future-of-jobs-report-2025/

About the Authors

Luis Javier Pentón Herrera, PhD, is an award-winning Spanish and English educator and a best-selling author. In 2024, he was selected as the TESOL Teacher of the Year, awarded by the TESOL International Association and National Geographic Learning. He is a professor at VIZJA University, in Poland, and his teaching and research projects are situated at the intersection of identity, emotions, and well-being in language and literacy education, social-emotional learning, autoethnography and storytelling, refugee education, and language weaponization. You can connect with Luis Javier on Instagram (@luisjavierpentonherrera) and on his website (luispenton.com).

Grazzia Maria Mendoza Chirinos, MEd, MA, is an award-winning educator with 32 years of experience in education. She was awarded the Virginia French Allen Award for Scholarship and Service in 2018 and the Outstanding Advocate Award in 2023. As a researcher at the University of Wisconsin Center for Education Research she developed the learning agenda for research to support educators and prioritized themes such as didactics, technology, and SEL. In addition, in her advocacy efforts, she contributes to highlighting women's empowerment narratives and decentering advocacy through global efforts. You can connect with Grazzia on LinkedIn (www.linkedin.com/in/grazzia-m-mendoza-ch-m-ed-264b5940).

About the Series Editor

Thomas S. C. Farrell, PhD, is a professor at Brock University, Canada. His professional interests include reflective practice and second language teacher education and development. He has published widely in these areas. His work can be found at www.reflectiveinquiry.ca.

See what else TESOL Press has to offer!

bookstore.tesol.org

www.ingramcontent.com/pod-product-compliance
Ingram Content Group UK Ltd.
Pitfield, Milton Keynes, MK11 3LW, UK
UKHW050411240426
12048UKWH00020B/1458